Waiter! Waiter!

words leslie falconer   pictures chris lensch

To my mom, who worked hard to teach me
to have good manners. - L.F.

To Kristen. - C.L.

First published by Experience Early Learning Company
7243 Scotchwood Lane, Grawn, Michigan 49637 USA

ISBN: 978-1-937954-08-6
visit us at **www.ExperienceEarlyLearning.com**

Waiter! Waiter!

words leslie falconer   pictures chris lensch

experience
Early Learning Company

waiter, waiter! I'd like some food,

so I'll try to not be rude.

I'll wash my hands before I eat,
wishy wash, wishy wishy wash.

Waiter, waiter! I'd like some food,

so I'll try to not be rude.

Burp!

I chew my food with my mouth closed
Mmm mm mm. Mm mm mm mmm.

waiter, waiter! I'd like some food,

so I'll try to not be rude.

I'll sit and wait, until you
take my plate.

19

Thank you very much!

20

Waiter! Waiter!

words leslie falconer   music brian steckler

CHORUS

Wai-ter, wai-ter, I'd like some food So I'll try____ to not_ be rude Wai - ter, wai - ter,____ can't__ you see__ You'll get no trou - ble____ from me____

VERSE 1

I'll wash my hands be-fore I__ eat Wi-shy wash, wi-shy wi-shy wash

CHORUS

Wai-ter, wai-ter, I'd like some food So I'll try____ to not_ be rude Wai - ter, wai - ter,____ can't__ you see__ You'll get no trou - ble____ from me____

24

experience
Early Learning Company

Experience Early Learning specializes in the development and publishing of research-based curriculum, books, music and authentic assessment tools for early childhood teachers and parents around the world. Our mission is to inspire children to experience learning through creative expression, play and open-ended discovery. We believe educational materials that invite children to participate with their whole self (mind, body and spirit) support on-going development and encourage children to become the authors of their own unique learning stories.

www.ExperienceEarlyLearning.com